Ribbon Without End

Ribbon Without End

Poems by

Dorothy Baird

Cover design by Shay Culligan

ISBN: 978-1-63980-130-5

Kelsay Books
502 South 1040 East, A-119
American Fork, Utah 84003
Kelsaybooks.com

In Memoriam
Nettie Boswell Sullivan Cook Baker
(1889–1973)
my feisty grandmother—confidant, teacher,
preserver of family stories

Acknowledgments

I am grateful to the editors of the following publications in which these poems have appeared, sometimes in slightly different forms.

Copperfield Review: "Arrival"
Hermit Feathers Review 2019: "Caves," "Grandmother's fountain
    pen," "night meditation"
Hermit Feathers Review 2020: "Dust"
Hermit Feathers Review 2021: "Sophie's Song: Growing Season,"
    "Haiku Mindset"
Heron Clan VI: "The Cedar Chest," "Disappearance of Matter,"
    "Minona," "Nobody's Favorite Uncle" (original title: "You May
    Know Him")
Indelible Ripples: "A Tale of Two Stories" (Aldrich Press, 2017)
Kakalak 17: "Life Lines"
Kakalak 18: "Water to Wine"
Kakalak 20: "Tea with Grandmother's Ghost"
Poets Facing the Wall: "In Concert"
Rose in the World: "Communion in the Dark"

A note of thanks to Jo Barbara Taylor, my editor and friend, to Sarah Edwards and all those whose insightful comments contributed to this work.

Contents

tall tales
about the past
infuse life in those long gone
could-have-been marries certainty
sparks legends, traditions

—db

Dust

I seldom dust high shelves.
Now and then, I climb a ladder,
make up for neglect.

At the top, rest photo albums,
redundant now, their contents stored
in digits—zeroes and ones—

collections of deckle-edged,
black and white snapshots,
concave in permanent curls,

cardboard frames border
sepia images, stoic faces
faded above rigid bodies.

Relatives preserved with paste,
tangible proof of existence
turning to dust.

Each album, an atlas,
maps that lead to my place
in this convex world.

Lost Stories

I sift through a mix of loose pictures:
Grim women held upright by corsets,
bearded men draped in watch chains.
I know dates—births, marriages, deaths.
Bare bones, all that remain.

I do not know their stories,
their work, how they bore up.
I imagine their passions:
   fear for drought-seared crops
   despair over empty bellies
   tears upon burying a child.

I do not know their stories,
their needs and desires,
the secrets they keep:
   joy at a soldier's return
   longing for love
   thrill of a furtive kiss.

I do not know the stories
buried at each death,
   forgotten.
I want to unravel their lives,
   bound in faded ribbon.

Arrival

(William, aboard the *Transport*, departed London, July 4, 1635)

At dawn our ship tacks into the James River,
heads northwest toward James Towne,
toward land promised me.

The *Transport* rocks under my feet,
the only sound, a steady swoosh
as prow pierces sun-glazed ripples.

The fertile scent of foliage lining both shores
revives me after weeks spent below deck
breathing the ship's stench.

A feast of August green feeds my hunger
for color after six weeks of blues—
sky, sea, night.

The King demands gold from these lands.
I shall find it on my grant,
whether I dig for it or grow it:

>   Maize, its colors hidden in silks and husks,
>   will rise from tilled soil, provide
>   grain for bread, fodder for animals.
>
>   Grape vines trellised on trees,
>   draped with clusters of purple-tinged amber,
>   will fill hogsheads with claret and port.
>
>   Tobacco's emerald fans will turn tan,
>   age to mahogany, deposit gold in my pocket,
>   before leaves disappear in curls of smoke.

I yearn for a landowner's life, no longer toiling
to fill another's purse. This night, God willing,
I'll feel my own property beneath my back.

Night Sounds in a Virgin Land

whirr, buzz, chirp, click
green fertile sounds

electric in night air
cicada, katydid, cricket, beetle

each small body quivers
in urgent calls for a mate

a language of courtship
that I can't decipher

no time for human preliminaries
no secret smiles, no whispered endearments

demands
rise and fall in waves

a pulse
pulse
pulse

Emily, 1776

I startle from sleep at the sound
of the stair's third step
squeaking under Isham's foot
as he comes to bed.

I reach out to him,
remember   he's gone soldiering.
The noisy step, a dreamed wish.
I sleep alone.

He joined fellow farmers,
seized with righteous fervor,
swore they'd rout the Red Coats
with muskets, sticks, and bricks.

Men, giddy with ideals,
made brave by indignation,
set out singing, rollicking,
boys playing war.

I'm angry with him,
King George and God.
Awake alone,
I ache for his voice, his touch,

I pray God will keep him
from musket balls, illness, capture.
I fear he'll not come home.

Communion in the Dark

The woodland trail
behind my house
pulls me outside.
Wearying monotony,
solitary life
suffocate me.

Nothing here is closed-up,
shut down, isolated:
squirrels sprint through trees
playing tag,
deer's hoof cracks
a brittle stick,
sparrow scolds the crow
too near her nest,
woodpecker hammers out
a burrow near the lowest limb
of the tallest tree
above the sun-soaked canopy.

Intent on what's above,
I miss what's at my feet,
stagger over ropes
of exposed roots,
each as thick as my wrist,
bulging beneath leafy mulch,
unruly warp and weft of forest floor.

I cannot see the work of roots:
they anchor one another,
sense a neighbor's need,
share their abundance,
bind together in dark oneness.

A Tale of Two Stories

Five generations handed down Mary's story.
Now her tale is mine to tell:
James, captain of a Confederate ship at Pensacola,
took a Yankee bullet, died a hero.

Mary's account promoted James to commander
though records show him a sixty-day recruit.
His raw Georgia company,
scantily trained, hopped up on rhetoric,
marched four hundred miles to Florida,
crossed the bay to capture Fort Pickens.

When the Rebs attacked
entrenched Union forces,
James was hit before his feet touched beach.
Buddies stacked his body like cord wood,
carted it home to his bride.

The widow and her infant Clara
slipped through streaming lines
of enemy soldiers
escaped
     established
James' blood line and legend,
a ribbon without end.

The Coleman Home

Riven by war when brother
fought brother, the family lost
its name on the battlefield.
Daughters struggle to scrabble
a living, sell off land bit by bit
to preserve their home.

Empty bellies force the women
to pack tools, china, mother's portrait,
hitch the mules, head west,
the house clouded by dust
from their wagon wheels
as failure clouds their minds.

They join cousins on the frontier,
turn their backs on the old life,
begin anew: take in boarders,
wash, cook, clean—hardly time
to think of life before.

The old house still stands,
grandeur gone, made shabby
by a jumble of hasty repairs.
Surnames of owners change
but Coleman lives in faint paint
on the gate like a grave marker.

The scarred front door,
cedar the color of cider,
still wears the old knocker,
monogramed with *C*,
a talisman against oblivion.

Restoration

As the day goes on
puffy clouds merge,
form thunderheads,
reduce bright day to grey.
No pinks and purples of twilight,
only roiling black
shrouds the sky,
threatens this land.

We, the people in peril,
cannot protect ourselves
against a force
that gathers power,
abides by no rules,
destroys all in its path
with fearsome lightening
resounding noise,

but some weather the worst,
believe the promise
of resilience after disaster,
rise above destruction,
resolve to rebuild
on firmer foundation.

We pray for tomorrow's
rosy dawn to grow brighter
until its rays sweep skies clean
like a broad broom
and free our land from disaster,
urge the least leaf to glisten.

Texas

(Mrs. Giles [Sallie Jane] Sullivan, 1887)

Mr. Sullivan is the new State Agent
for Cole Bros. Lightning Rods,
so we're moving. Packed up, sold off,
boarded the train for New Orleans
where we'll transfer to the Star & Crescent for Texas,
    Horace, no running in the aisle!
where the boys hope to see Indians
so they practice quick draws,
use their fingers for six-shooters
holstered in their pockets,
    Shhh, boys! Don't be so noisy.
while Minona, our oldest, reads stories to the girls,
who play with toddler Perry and baby Aussie,
    Girls, let the baby sleep.
as Mr. Sullivan reads newspapers, studies maps,
plans sales routes, talks about our new life,
    Minona, get your sister a drink of water.
but I'm tired from staying up nights with the baby,
packing trunks, keeping eight children corralled,
    Mr. Sullivan, please settle your sons.
so I try to nap but can't
because I think of family in Holly Springs,
which makes me cry,
especially Mother who's right mad
at Mr. Sullivan for taking us to the wild west,
but I'm anxious to see the city of Austin,
after living in small-town Mississippi with only
relatives for friends, yet I think to myself,
    Oh, Mr. Sullivan, this is hard.

Handing Down

(Sallie Jane, 1892)

The tin box, gold scrolls and fancy letters,
       smells of long-gone tea
       and must from old buttons.

Little Perry pops open the tight-fitting lid,
       colors and shapes spill, bounce,
       settle in a heap on the braided rug.

He groups them at my feet
       as I mend and tell stories
       about each saved button.

Crocheted balls, celadon green,
       waltzed down my dress when I met Papa,
       so tiny a dozen fit in the small boy's hand.

Brass ones worn by grandfather, a lieutenant,
       knew the smell of gunpowder,
       heard the blast and whirr of bullets.

Shoe buttons survived from the boots
       we girls wore, one after another,
       until they gave way, fell apart.

Wooden toggles carved by Uncle Jack's hand
       while at sea, to clasp a cloak
       under his sweetheart's chin.

I fasten my son to the past with buttons.

In Concert

Redwoods
Shallow roots wide
Twine with others underground
Brawny network withstands tempest
In unison   Might

Giles Teaches His Sons to Sell Lightning Rods

(1895)

Boys, hitch up the wagon,
study its fancy lettering.
That sign says it all:

Cole Bros.
Lightning Rods
The Best on Earth
All Work Done Scientifically

Drive into the country.
When you come to a farmhouse,
stop under a shade tree,
inspect your horses' hooves,
remove a pebble or two.

When the farmer comes out,
talk about the weather,
such as,
Early heat this spring.
Summer's on its way.

Ask for a cup of water.
Talk about the weather,
such as,
Your soil looks mighty dry.
You must be hoping for rain.

He'll ask about your sign,
about lightning rods:
How *do they work?*
      You tell him.

Never seen one up close.
      You show him.
Do they really work?
      You assure him.

Now here's where you talk science:
mention Ben Franklin, the kite,
the key, the famous invention.
Cole Bros., maker and distributor.
Tell him about "scientific" installation.

Remind him thunderheads
will roam the skies
their fiery strikes burning down
unprotected barns.
Tell him these rods
are "the best on earth."

When he asks
How much?
      You tell him.
Add,
      For what it does, it's cheap.

When he balks,
talk paying-on-time,
and estimate his cost of rebuilding.

Then, boys, you've made a sale!

A Boat Becomes a Home

(Austin, Texas)

I. The Boat (1900)

Parasoled ladies and high-collared men,
enjoy spring breezes as the paddle wheeler
steams across Lake McDonald.
Flirtatious couples dine in elegance,
two-step to syncopated Ragtime,
Camel Walk, Turkey Trot, Bunny Hug,
and waltz to a five-piece band.
An April storm cancels excursions.
The empty boat rides mounting swells
until record rain forces failure of the dam.
Unbound, the river sweeps downstream.
Grey, roiling waters lift the boat, hurl it bankside.
Flood recedes, reveals mud-mired remains.

II. The Home (Flores Street, 1901)

A builder finds the boat's beached timbers
a source of lumber to construct a house
for Giles' family of twelve, who desire
the latest luxuries: screened windows and doors,
gas lights, indoor plumbing, porcelain bathtub.
Giles adds a lightning rod from his stock
to protect against the orange tongue of fire.
The Sullivans celebrate New Year's at home.
After a dinner of ham and black-eyed peas
for good luck, the oldest son cranks the Victrola,
others push back furniture, roll up the rug.
Giles and Sallie Jane waltz in wide circles.
Above, a copper finial pierces blue heavens,
ready to send danger into red soil below.

Haiku Mindset

1.

small lizard disguised
as begonia's glossy leaf
watches from safety

2.

morning mist conjures
redbud's purple blooms   neon
float beside dogwood

3.

clouds squeeze out showers
no drama of sound or light
Soft plups fill puddles

4.

child walks between parents
curls legs makes their arms a swing
memories of daughter

5.

under the covers
your sleeping hand finds mine
fingers remember   curl

The Cedar Chest

(Nettie, 1911)

For my sixteenth birthday,
Brother builds a chest of cedar
to hold my needlework.
I dream fairy-tale tomorrows
as my needle
  loops pink and purple lazy daisies,
  chains green vines on flour-sack towels,
  marks cross-stitches on gingham aprons.
I arrange them in the cedar scent
of a crisp, green future,
the chest as big as our Sunday table.

At eighteen,
I dream happily-ever-after,
long to become
mistress of my own home,
  embroider bed linens,
  tat lace for nightgowns,
  monogram handkerchiefs.
I wrap them in tissue,
layer with lavender,
stack in the chest
as big as a bed.

At twenty-two,
ready to live my dream,
I carry my handkerchief
down the aisle,
nightgown packed in a valise.
My husband has no time for me.

I unpack alone:
      linens with my needlework,
      wedding gifts—china, silver,
      rolling pin, and pots.
The empty chest now yawns
as big as a tomb.

Giles' Lament

(1914)

I buried Sallie Jane a year ago,
  our children have flown
    with children of their own,
      leaving emptiness.

A muscular silence elbows aside
  echoes of shouts, quarrels, giggles
    the melodies of life
      that filled these rooms.

Gone are the small noises that attended
  Sallie each day, the sounds I treasure:
    hymns hummed
      clatter of shoes on stairs
        chime of cup on saucer.

I no longer hear her music,
  not even in my mind's ear.

Minona

(1915)

I am the first-born of ten.
Mother births and nurses.
Father travels
I keep house
hold hands of toddlers,
teach manners and the ABC's,
patch hand-me-downs
until threadbare with wear.

Mother sickens, I tend her
then plan the funeral,
run father's house.
The daily routine,
the weekly schedule
leave no time for friends,
socials or dancing.
Some call me selfless,
but I envision a life of my own,
and their good intentions
echo in my emptiness.

Brothers and sisters write
of jobs, families. I live
in the slipstream of their lives.

Death and Mistletoe

(Sophie, 1938)

The Christmas before we married
      Austin gave me a ball of mistletoe
      tied with scarlet ribbon,
says, *For you, my sweet Sophie.*

Every Christmas, he fashions a kissing ball
      cut from the tree outside our home,
      the house that was a boat.
says, *For stealing kisses from my sweet Sophie.*

His mother Sallie brought that tree, a seedling,
      from Mississippi. She fussed over it,
      watched it grow a foot a year,
said, *A transplant, just like me.*

Today, Austin heads out
      with ladder and butcher knife
      to cut back the mistletoe,
says, *Parasites suck life out of the hackberry.*

He reaches, the ladder sways.
      It falls one way, Austin another.
      I find him in a spreading scarlet stain,
say, *My Austin's gone.*

Sophie's Song: Growing Season

I bury my grief from Austin's death bringing life
from fecund soil like a garden midwife.

I yearn to work the dirt, to seed in rows
in early spring when sun first warms the earth,

Swiss chard, green peas and beets in dark repose,
their sprouts to join bright blooms in annual rebirth.

My fork amends the soil, composes fertile humus.
I plant, spread mulch, water well and wait,

find joy in heads of nodding sprout's lush newness.
I weed and watch the coaxing sun create

the leaves of mint, of sage, the hanging shells
of trellised beans, and jeweled globes of garnet,

amber, emerald tied to stakes like bells,
and buried deep, carrots and bulbs of garlic.

Water, toil and sun on soil, a golden alchemy,
lifts me above the dross of my own reality.

Grandmother's fountain pen

green, marbled, trimmed with gold,
gift from her second husband,
the one who loved her,
sleeps in my drawer.

An atrophied bladder of dry ink
no longer bleeds on the page.
Its case bears still the stigmata
where the stub of a finger
rested after the spider bite.

Once she sat in the chair
that rocked her babies, rocked
her like the ships that bore them away.
While I played at her feet,

she penned courage to her sons,
strewn 'round the world by war,
addressed thin blue envelopes with care
lest letters and numbers bleed.

She wrote to their wives
perseverance and prayers,
remedies for colic,
stories of her sons as boys.

Though her hand has stilled,
I hold the pen and feel its warmth,
hear her wisdom.

The Importance of Small

At six I ask where the stars end.
Everything I know has an end:
books, my room, our house, our town.

Maps show borders for states, countries,
but the starry night goes on and on,
so big, a spaceship can't find its edge,

yet I am so little, not even a speck
in a universe with no limits.

In science class, I learn the sun is a star,
move from Styrofoam balls hanging on string
to galaxies, white dwarfs, black holes,

and measurements devised to gauge immensity
gigantic past grasp but not boundless,
finite in the infinite, just like me

just like the very tiny.
Without particles, vastness is void.

Nobody's Favorite Uncle

after Thomas Lux's "Guide to the Perpetually Perplexed"

He is not perplexed, neither perpetually nor occasionally,
but knows his mind, expresses it on all subjects,
spouts opinion as firm fact in declarative sentences.
Large black periods splatter everywhere.

Like yeasty bread dough, the dots rise
into exclamation points, put an end to conversation.
Uncle stands on a soapbox to elevate his views,
rolls each word like honey on the tongue

though others hear the rasp of sandpaper.
Verbs like *love* and *hate,* leave no room
for complications or extenuations,
clamp his views like a vise.

Life Lines

A photograph of mother sits on my desk.
Wrinkles plow her brow,
at the center, an incised scowl line—
tailings that reflect a life

of pinch and strain raising children
in a house of indignity and injury
from an indiscreet husband and
her father's lingering damage.

She leans into the camera,
crinkling eyes add crow's feet,
forced smile, laugh lines, but
they do not eclipse the past.

I long to trace
each seam with my fingers,
smooth each trough
deep in skin and muscle

as a Japanese kintsugi master repairs
priceless porcelain shards
with ribbons of gold
to mend brokenness.

Disappearance of Matter

after Lynn Emanuel's "These Days,"

Goldfinch splash in a bowl
beside my dogwood,
then spread wings and fly.
Water gone but grit,
a bathtub ring, persists.

Mother drums her fingers on white satin.

Leaves flutter spirals
to earth. Withered,
the color of old age,
they crackle and crunch
shatter to silence as soil.

Mother tosses her head on the pillow.

Nails, buried in dirt, spill out
as I repot my jade plant.
Specters now, inert power gone,
rusty frays where iron
leached out for emerald leaves.

Mother mutters in coffin-muted voice.

Fire levels acres of forest.
No trees sway
or branches sigh,
only ashes, the matter of death,
minerals for new life.

Mother sits up in her grave,
says, *I hate this poem.*
I will never leave you.

Dust Motes in an Empty House

My hands shadow the window,
touch grimy panes, shield the glare
as I peer into a sunlit room, empty
yet scared from the past.

Despite attempts to paint them away,
the front windowsill, the height
of my four-year-old mouth,
still wears the imprint of tiny teeth.

Cupped floorboards raked
by my chair's broken castor
bear an unrepaired gash,
the air still holds my scolding.

Inside, I breathe must and dust, vision
the rooms furnished and peopled as before:

>   Daddy sits in the nubby green chair
>   beside the refrigerator-sized radio, listens
>   to news, rattles a copy of the *News Herald*.
>   No talking between six and six-thirty.

>   The sweet, yeasty aroma of dinner rolls
>   drifts on the oven's radiating warmth
>   while Mommy fries chicken, tends greens.
>   My mouth waters—even now.

>   I address thirty-for-a-half-dollar valentines amid
>   crepe paper scraps, glue, scissors and my glorious
>   red fringed shoe box covered with hearts,
>   the top slit to receive messages of love.

I'm seeing the phantom of a happy day,
but other specters echo—angry voices,
gritted teeth, slammed doors—the soundtrack
that raised fear and wounded my heart.

The grace of time and understanding
produces forgiveness, dims memories,
though like painted-over teeth marks,
they don't completely disappear.

night meditation

everything sleeps
even the moon rests
under a cloak of clouds

gives no glimmer to catch
on gardenia petals
thick as flesh

gives no fire to ignite
the orange glow
of Chinese lanterns

the woods beyond
a saturated blotter
lacks color   depth   details of trees

receives nor releases light
admits nothing except the scent
of lavender   exhaled by the garden

cleaving the air   releasing recollection
of the linen closet (where I hid
as a kid, wanting to be found)

when the moon rests
I walk the garden
slipping into the stream of memory

Caves

I first learned cave magic
when grandmother draped
blankets over furniture,
created a snug space for us
to eat crustless sandwiches,
share stories, tell secrets
(sometimes just pss, pss, pssss).

At sixteen, I didn't need a hide-away,
but a haven. Grandmother spread
comfort over me. In safety, I shared
joys, mistakes, fears and tears.
She listened to what I said,
heard what I couldn't say,
became my solid ground.

Today, I remember how it's done:
draped blankets, fancy sandwiches,
crawl with my granddaughter
into our own magic. Planting
seeds, I tell her stories, secrets
(pss, pss, pssss),
listen to her.

continuum

one moment
leads to another
yesterday vanished
from present
future spools out
like a ribbon
a stream with no end

Tea with Grandmother's Ghost

(Nettie Sullivan Baker, 1889–1973)

I fill your hand-painted plate with cinnamon cookies,
the ones I learned to make standing on a chair at your elbow:
      sift flour gently
      measure precisely
      pack brown sugar tightly

You sit at my table set with your linen, your plate, your cookies.
Old pictures rest between us and I beg you to tell the stories:

      how Clara, the grandmother of my grandfather,
      escaped war ahead of marching soldiers' drums
      to give her baby safety in the west

      about the chest your brothers built for you,
      how its cedar seeped into your linens
      became the scent of hope

      the tales of each button in your mother's tin box,
      the small ones she wore when she met your papa,
      the shiny ones from soldiers' jackets

You give me glimpses of how our people lived,
but can you tell me how it is for them now,
how will it be for me?

Will I think about those still living,
will I feel comfort or regret,
can you tell me now,
or will answers birth at my death?

About the Author

Dorothy Baird taught in the English Department of Western Connecticut University and was Managing Editor of *Heat Treating*, a journal serving a facet of the steel industry. Her poetry has appeared in the chapbook *Indelible Ripples* (Aldrich Press, 2017), as well as in journals and anthologies. Baird is grateful for the experiences of making her home in multiple cities across the country, reflecting her ancestors' migration recorded in *Ribbon Without End*. She has settled with her husband and dog Parker in Chapel Hill, North Carolina.

www.ingramcontent.com/pod-product-compliance
Lightning Source LLC
Chambersburg PA
CBHW071751090426
42738CB00011B/2649